Animal Senses

Shelly C. Buchanan, M.S.

Consultant

Leann Iacuone, M.A.T., NBCT, ATC
Riverside Unified School District

Publishing Credits

Rachelle Cracchiolo, M.S.Ed., *Publisher*
Conni Medina, M.A.Ed., *Managing Editor*
Diana Kenney, M.A.Ed., NBCT, *Senior Editor*
Dona Herweck Rice, *Series Developer*
Robin Erickson, *Multimedia Designer*
Timothy Bradley, *Illustrator*

Image Credits: Cover, p. 1 Shutterstock; pp. 3, 4, 9, 18, 19, 20, 24,25, 26, 31, 32 iStock; pp. 17, 27 Juniors Bildarchiv GmbH / Alamy; p. 23 Karl H. Switak / Science Source; p. 17 MOB IMAGES / Alamy; 19 Omikron / Science Source; 25 Rod Planck / Science Source; p. 6 Stephen Frink Collection / Alamy; p. 21 The Natural History Museum / Alamy; pp. 11, 15 Timothy J. Bradley; all other images from Shutterstock.

Library of Congress Cataloging-in-Publication Data

Buchanan, Shelly, author.
    Animal senses / Shelly C. Buchanan.
        pages cm
    Summary: "Smell, sight, sound, touch, and taste . . . these are our senses. They help us understand the world around us. But what about animals? Do cats taste ice cream? Can fish hear sounds underwater? Which animal smells with its tongue? Learn more about how animals sense the world around them."-- Provided by publisher.
    Audience: Grades 4 to 6.
    Includes index.
    ISBN 978-1-4807-4678-7 (pbk. : alk. paper)
1. Senses and sensation--Juvenile literature. 2. Physiology--Juvenile literature. 3. Animals--Juvenile literature. I. Title.
    QP431.B78 2016
    573.8'7--dc23
                                    2014045243

Teacher Created Materials

5301 Oceanus Drive
Huntington Beach, CA 92649-1030
http://www.tcmpub.com

ISBN 978-1-4807-4678-7

Table of Contents

Amazing Abilities

Have you ever wished you could smell an apple pie from miles away? What if you could use your feet to listen to your favorite song on the radio? Well, grizzly bears can smell a dead animal up to 20 kilometers (12 miles) away! And African elephants can use their feet to feel **vibrations** over 10 km (6 mi.) away! But don't despair. Even though you can't do those things, you have something in common with these animals.

Humans have five senses. We use our noses to smell food, and our mouths taste it. We use our hands to touch and feel if objects are sharp or soft. Our ears let us hear if danger is coming or if someone is singing a song. Our eyes let us see how amazing our world is. We use our senses to take in information about the world. Our brains process this information, and then our bodies respond to it. Our five senses help us understand and live in the world. Our senses have **adapted** to receive the information we need most.

A grizzly bear's sense of smell is seven times better than a bloodhound's.

A Stellar Skill Set

The hammerhead shark is a fearsome hunter. When a shark's around, every ocean animal is on high alert.

Shark noses are extra large for the ultimate smelling power. They can smell a single drop of blood in a swimming pool.

It's hard to escape from this shark's 270-degree **field of vision**.

270 degrees

Sharks can detect electricity—exactly like the kind produced when a fish twitches its muscles.

Most animals have the same five senses. Some even have more! But animals live in environments very different from our own. So their senses have developed to help them survive where they live. The results are amazing!

Eyes Have It

Sight is the most powerful human sense. We use it to move through the world during our waking hours. Most animals enjoy the use of sight, too! They use this sense to capture prey, escape predators, find mates, and move around. This all sounds familiar, right? Many animals, however, see the world very differently than we do.

To see, we open our eyes and move them in their sockets. But birds' eyes work differently. They don't move at all. To see beyond what's right in front of them, birds move their necks instead of their eyes.

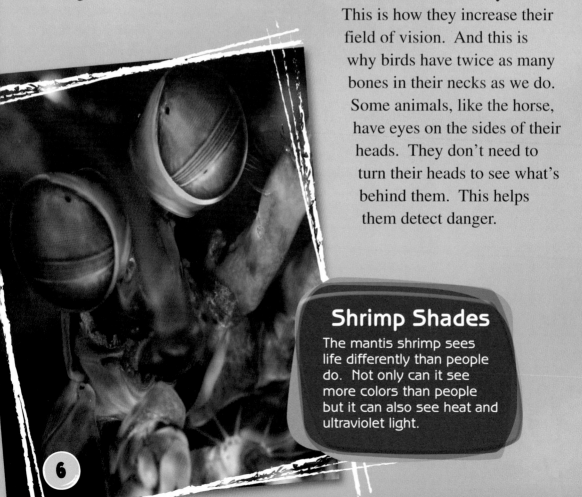

This is how they increase their field of vision. And this is why birds have twice as many bones in their necks as we do. Some animals, like the horse, have eyes on the sides of their heads. They don't need to turn their heads to see what's behind them. This helps them detect danger.

Shrimp Shades

The mantis shrimp sees life differently than people do. Not only can it see more colors than people but it can also see heat and ultraviolet light.

Owls can turn their heads around 270 degrees. They can turn their heads almost completely upside down!

Seeing Things Differently

Chameleons have eyelids that cover most of their eye with only a small hole for them to see through. Not only do these eyes have a 360-degree field of vision that allows them to see in every direction, but they can also move on their own. The chameleon can look forward with one eye...and backward with the other!

Most predatory animals, such as wolves, have eyes at the front of their head, which allow them to see straight ahead. This is called *binocular vision*. Both eyes look at the same thing, at the same time. This placement of the eyes is especially suited for predators who are attempting to capture prey. Other animals, like rabbits, have eyes on the sides of their heads. This allows them to have a wider field of vision so they can see incoming predators. This is called *monocular vision*. One eye sees one view and the other eye sees another view.

Some animals, like cats and owls, are able to see better in the dark than humans do. These animals are nocturnal. They sleep in the day and are awake at night. Their eyes have adapted to the dark so they can hunt prey. Most animals have two kinds of **cells** in their eyes: rods and cones. The rods are good for seeing in the dark. The cones are good for seeing color. Cats and owls have more rods than cones. They see well in the dark. But they don't see much color.

Rods and Cones

Dogs have more rods than cones in their eyes. They're missing the cones to see certain colors—so they can't see red or bright green!

human's vision

dog's vision

The Perfect Pupil?

The shape of an animal's eyes often reflects where it lives, when it is active, and what it's looking for.

A long, thin dark line lies at the center of a nocturnal gecko's eye. A small slit blocks out sunlight so these creatures aren't blinded during the day. The shape of their **pupil** gives them clearer vision—like a sharp TV screen. At night, their pupils expand to let in more light.

Owls have big, round pupils. Since owls are active at night, they need to be able to see in the dark.

The pupil grows larger at night to let in light. Their large eyes are filled with rods, so they can see and hunt in the dark. During the day, owls usually keep their eyes half closed.

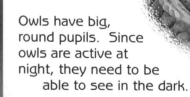

Hear Ye! Hear Ye!

Roar! The living world is a noisy place. People use sound to communicate and share ideas. We sing, laugh, and shout. Just like humans, many animals are very sensitive to sound. They use it to detect approaching predators, locate food and water, and communicate with other animals. Sound is made up of waves of energy moving through air, water, and other objects. Animals sense this energy as vibrations they feel or sounds they hear.

Animal ears come in all shapes and sizes in order to hear certain vibrations. There are teeny-tiny feather-covered holes on birds and gigantic earflaps on elephants. It's important for rabbits to hear if a predator is coming, so they have very long ears. Jackrabbit ears measure half the length of the rabbit's body. Ears can be found in some unusual places, too. Some insects, such as crickets, have ears on their legs. Some, such as hawk moths, have ears in their mouths!

To help them hear, fish use small hairs on their scales (shown here magnified) to feel the pressure in water created by sound waves.

Many animals can hear sounds that are too low or too high for our ears. Have you ever heard a dog bark for no apparent reason? It probably heard something you couldn't. Many animals can also move their ears in several directions. This allows them to better direct sounds into their ears—and to their brains.

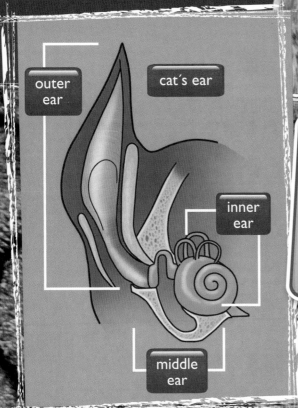

outer ear

cat's ear

inner ear

middle ear

Keep Your Balance

A cat has canals in its ears lined with hairs and liquid. The liquid in the canals allows the cat to know which direction it's facing, even if it's upside down! Its ears, combined with its flexible spine, allow it to land on its feet after most falls.

For some animals, hearing is even more important than seeing. Bats hunt for food at night. They catch most of the insects they eat in the air. Despite poor eyesight, these creatures spin and swerve nimbly. They avoid obstacles like trees and wires as they speed after their prey. Echolocation (ek-oh-loh-KEY-shuhn) helps bats know where they are and what's around them. Bats give off sound too high for people to hear. This sound bounces off nearby objects and animals. The echo helps bats know what's around, including their prey. They can even hear an echo bouncing off a mosquito's wing!

Dolphins and whales use echolocation, too. These ocean creatures send out whistles, squeaks, and clicks. Dolphins and whales have two to three times more nerves in their ears than humans. This allows them to be super-listeners. They hear sounds we can't.

The clicks made by sperm whales are the loudest and deepest made by any animal. The sounds bounce off obstacles, fish, and other creatures. These creatures of the deep use echolocation to travel, hunt, and avoid danger.

Playing Catch

Bats have ears shaped like funnels to help them catch the sound produced when they echolocate. They also have a flap in their ear to direct the sound. It's like a baseball glove for sound!

A High-Pitched Hello

Sound is measured in waves per second. One unit is called a hertz (Hz). People hear sounds between 20 and 20,000 Hz. Dolphins hear the highest sounds. They hear up to 150,000 Hz!

Sound travels at about 344 meters (376 yards) per second.

Whose Nose Knows?

For many animals, a keen sense of smell is a matter of life or death. A scent in the air or water carries a lot of information. Even in very small amounts, chemicals that make up an odor can be helpful. Animals use their sniffers to locate food or prey. They also use their noses to avoid predators. The right scent can even help animals find a mate.

There are some amazing noses in the animal kingdom. Consider an elephant's nose. It averages 2 meters (6.5 feet) in length! This terrific trunk is a super-sniffer. It also doubles as a useful tool. It can hold gallons of water and pick up heavy tree limbs.

Male moths boast one of the greatest senses of smell. They use their **antennae** to notice female moths up to six miles away. An octopus uses its tentacles to smell. A catfish uses its whiskers to "sniff" around. A snake uses its tongue to grab scent particles right out of the air!

male moth

A Sensitive Sniffer

Dogs have highly sensitive noses that can be trained to find many things from bees to DVDs to cancer. How do they do it?

A dog's nose is lined with millions of **receptors** that take in smells and send them to the brain.

Air enters a dog's nostrils. It leaves through the side of the nose. That keeps the incoming air pure for maximum smelling!

A dog processes smells in the olfactory bulb, a part of the brain that tells the dog what it's smelling and how to respond.

The human brain is 10 times larger than a dog's brain. But a dog has an olfactory bulb that is 3 times larger than a human's.

15

You probably talk to or e-mail your friends to see how they're doing. You might ask them questions, listen, and look at them. But do you ever sniff your friends to catch up? This is one way animals talk to one another. They send and receive information through smell. Think of a skunk. When you or other animals catch a whiff, the skunk's message comes through loud and clear: stay away! A skunk's scent serves as a powerful form of communication and protection.

A lot of other animals use their scent like a "Keep Out" sign, as well. Gorillas, foxes, and wild cats are just a few that do this. They urinate on trees or rocks to mark their territory. This lets other animals know that the land is already occupied. Visitors are NOT welcome!

Tell Me Everything

Animals use smell to communicate, not only with one another but also with you, too! When you're upset or scared, your pet can smell it. Your pets can know what mood you're in without you having to say a word.

Other animals use scents like a party invitation. When one ant finds food, the whole gang is invited! Ants pass scent messages to one another with their antennae. They also leave a trail of scent on the ground. This way, other ants can easily find the feast.

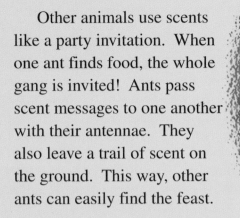

green ants

When a bee stings an animal or a person, it releases chemicals that other bees can smell. This lets them know there is danger in the area.

Bunting

When cats rub their heads against something, it's called *bunting*. This lets them mark their personal scent on family members, close friends, and treasured items. It's a kitty compliment!

Tongues for Tasting

What are your favorite foods? Why is it that you enjoy some foods more than others? It might be because of the texture of the food or the color. But you probably like it mostly because of the way it tastes. Many animals are sensitive to taste, too. Some have favorite foods. Many have foods they won't touch. Some are so particular they'll eat only one kind of food.

Different species have different taste buds in order to better detect the food they need to eat. Some use their taste buds to help them know what to avoid. Bitterness can be a sign that a type of food is poisonous. Sweetness can be a sign that a food will give animals a quick jolt of energy.

Taste buds are sensory **organs**. These are the receptors that tell the brain whether a food is salty, sour, sweet, or bitter. Scientists think most animals experience tastes the same way people do. But it's difficult to know!

Meow!

Cats can't taste sweetness at all. They lost this ability long ago. While your kitten may lap up the water you dish out, don't give your cat any ice cream. This favorite treat of humans would be wasted on cats!

bitter

Taste It All

Contrary to popular belief, sweet, sour, salty, bitter, and savory are all tastes that can be sensed by all parts of your tongue. The only exception being that the back of your tongue is especially sensitive to bitter tastes. This is to urge people to spit out things that may be poisonous or spoiled.

Test your Taste Buds

People can have anywhere from 2,000 to 8,000 taste buds. Find out if you have a lot or a little with a simple at home experiment.

1. Put two drops of blue food coloring on your tongue and swallow a few times.

2. Check your tongue to see how blue it is. If it's really blue, you have fewer taste buds. A pink tongue means you have a lot!

taste buds magnified

In humans, taste buds are found on the tongue. But insects like butterflies use their feet to taste things! They walk on flowers to decide if they want the nectar. Their tongues remain neatly rolled up under their heads and then spring out to suck up nectar. These creatures taste sweetness 200 times more strongly than we do!

A snake tastes things by grabbing scent particles out of the air with its tongue. It presses these particles into a space on the roof of its mouth. This nook, called *Jacobson's organ*, sends a message to its brain with the scent information.

Humans have 2 to 8 thousand taste buds on their tongues. A **carnivore** has fewer. For instance, a lion has about 470. It eats a simple diet of meat and more meat. It doesn't need to have a wide range of tastes. And the few foods this animal does eat tend to be pretty safe. An **omnivore** has more taste buds. A pig clocks in at 15,000. It needs to find a wider variety of food. An **herbivore** has the most taste buds. A cow has 25,000! It needs to locate a lot of different flavors to meet its dietary needs. An herbivore also tends to have more taste buds so it can detect dangerous chemicals in plants.

For the Win!

Catfish take the cake for the largest number of taste buds. They have about 175,000! They are located in the catfish's mouth and on its skin and whiskers. With so many taste buds, the catfish can find food in dark water.

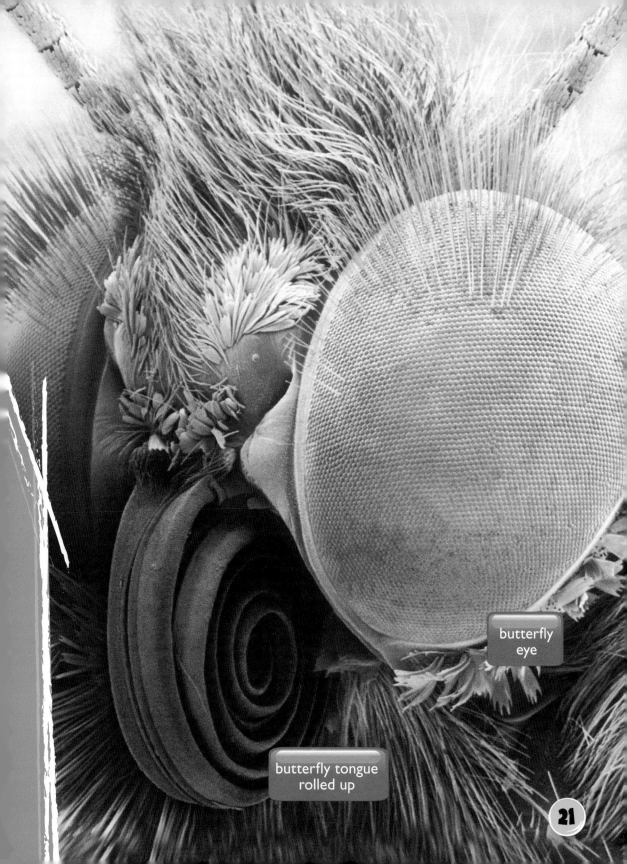

butterfly eye

butterfly tongue rolled up

Touch & Feel

You use your sense of touch to make your bed, eat a snack, write a note, and cuddle an animal. You might also use this sense to avoid danger, such as a hot stove. Most animals have developed a sense of touch for the same reasons. Their sense of touch allows them to build a home, find food, communicate, and stay safe. Animals have developed a variety of touch organs to help them survive.

Walruses hunt for food by rubbing their heads in the mud. They use the whiskers around their mouths to feel for food. They can easily detect something, such as a crab or a clam, that has the right shape and texture for eating. Then, they dig in for lunch!

A giant anteater can barely see. But it does have a super-nose for finding insects. When its extra-long tongue goes to work, it can extend deep inside an ant nest. The sticky saliva acts like glue. The giant anteater's tongue can slurp up 25,000 insects a day!

giant anteater

Hot Lips

Snakes have gaps around their lips that allow them to feel nearby heat. These gaps are called *heat pits*. They alert the snake to warm-blooded prey ready for the taking. Can you say "dinnertime"?

Humans aren't the only animals that use touch to say hello. Apes and monkeys hug and sometimes kiss when they meet one another.

An animal's sense of touch can keep it safe and sound. Many kinds of fish swim in groups for safety. They move together like dancers. To do this, they use their lateral line system. A fish has one lateral line on each side of its body. It includes receptors that sense pressure. When a neighbor fish moves, the others can sense it in a split second. They move with it. Moving together, the fish find safety in numbers.

Star-nosed moles are nearly blind. So, they have evolved an incredible sense of touch. These moles have 22 soft tentacles surrounding their noses. These tentacles carry 25,000 touch **sensors**. The sensors are more sensitive than human fingers! Moles use these sensors to find their way through the dark. They hunt for food this way, too. They also use this super-sense to avoid going out into the open where they might be attacked by predators.

Other animals rely on being untouchable. Porcupines sport prickly spines to keep enemies away. Bees and wasps use their sharp stingers to ward off enemies.

A Tricky Touch

When you touch something, electrical signals are sent to your brain. Scientists monitored monkeys' brains and watched where signals were sent when the monkeys were touched. Then, they sent an electrical signal to that part of the brain but didn't touch the monkeys! The monkeys reacted as if they were touched.

star-nosed mole

Hunting by Touch

Like the star-nosed mole, the water shrew relies entirely on touch to hunt. It doesn't use smell, sight, or hearing to guide it. Instead, its whiskers help it locate food underwater.

water shrew

Power of Information

Every animal, from a tiny ant to a gigantic whale, needs to receive and process information about the world. While many animals have the same five senses as people, some have developed additional senses that are hard for us to imagine. Sights, sounds, smells, tastes, electrical pulses, and more all provide animals with information. And the brain lies at the center of it all, taking in sensory details and telling the body how to respond. The way each animal receives information and uses it may differ. That's because the world looks, sounds, tastes, and feels different to every living thing. But every creature uses its senses to make sense of the world!

common squirrel monkey

A Sense of Humor

Humor isn't like the other senses. It doesn't give us information about the world. But it definitely affects the way we see the world! Rats, dogs, and gorillas have all been seen doing something that looks very similar to laughing. And crows have even been caught playing pranks on one another!

Think Like a Scientist

How does the shape of an animal's body parts relate to its abilities? Experiment and find out!

What to Get

- 4 sheets of paper
- music
- scissors
- tape

What to Do

1. Roll the paper into a cone shape. Make the smaller end fit snuggly around your ear. Tape the paper together.

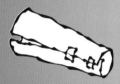

2. Hold the smaller end of the cone to your ear. Plug the other ear with a finger. Listen to music.

3. Now switch the direction of the cone. Listen again. What do you notice? Experiment with different ear shapes.

4. Next, hold two sheets of paper on either side of your face. Try to look around without moving your head. What type of animal may have vision similar to this?

5. Take two sheets of paper and cut long slits so you can barely see through them. Hold them up to your eyes and look around. How well can you see?

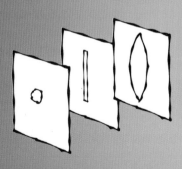

6. Cut the slits wider so you can see a bit more. How does your vision change? Experiment with different eye shapes. What animals have these eyes?

Glossary

adapted—changed so that it is easier to live in a particular place

antennae—thin, sensitive organs on the head of an insect, crab, etc., which are used mainly to feel and touch things

carnivore—a living thing that only eats meat

cells—basic units of life

field of vision—the area that you can see without moving your eyes

herbivore—a living thing that only eats plants

omnivore—a living thing that eats both plants and animals

organs—parts of the body that have particular functions

pupil—the small, black, round area at the center of the eye

receptors—nerve endings that sense changes in light, temperature, pressure, etc., and cause the body to react in a particular way

sensors—devices that detect or sense heat, light, sound, motion, etc., and then react to it in a particular way

vibrations—rapid motions of particles back and forth

Index

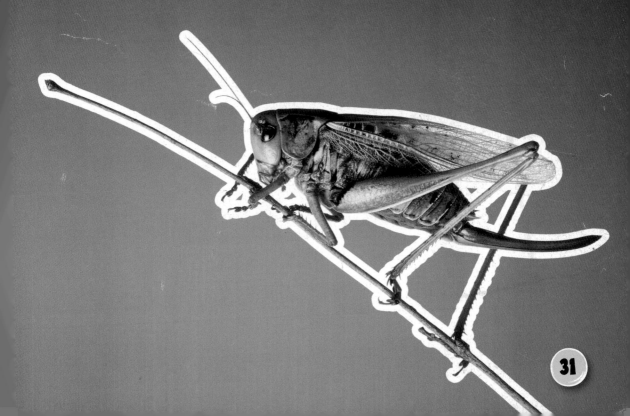

Your Turn!

Night Lights

Next time you're out at night, take time to listen to all the sounds around you. Smell the air. Use your hands to feel around you. Now, imagine being a nocturnal animal. Think about how you could use your senses to find food and stay safe.